Discover Writing Discover Korea 7

[여는 말]

한국에는 수준 높은 좋은 영어 교재들이 많이 있습니다. 그러나 이들 중 대부분의 책들은 한국 학생들의 삶과 문화에 진정으로 연결되어 있지 않고, 외국 문화와 맥락으로 가득 차 있습니다. 학생들이 교재의 내용에 공감하지 못해 영어에 대한 관심을 잃는 것을 보며 이러한 의문들이 들기 시작했습니다. "만약 한국 문화를 중심으로 한 교제가 있다면 어떨까?", "만약 교재가 학생들의 일상 생활과 더 밀접하게 연결되어 있다면 어떨까?".

이렇게 시작된 "만약"은 "나도 어쩌면 작은 변화를 가져올 수 있다."는 생각의 씨앗이 되었습니다. 모든 것을 바꿀 방법은 없을지도 모르지만, 제가 시작점이 되어 한국 학생들을 위한, 한국 문화를 반영한 영어 학습 자료, 그리고 학생들에게 친숙하고 위로가 되는 학습자료를 제공하고 싶었습니다.

Discover Writing Discover Korea 시리즈는 **총 10 권**으로 구성되어 있습니다. 이 시리즈는 제목에서도 선명하게 보이듯이 영어 글쓰기를 위한 책입니다. 이 10 권의 책시리즈들은 **각 장르별 영어 글쓰기 스킬을 제공**하면서 동시에 **다른 책에서 다루지 않는 문법의 일면들을 제공**하고 있습니다. 이 책을 통해 또한 **학생들은 자기평가가 가능**합니다. 보통의 교실환경에서 학생들은 주로 평가를 받는 입장입니다. 학생들은 점수에만 매인 채 평가의 의미와 결과의 이유는 잘 알지 못합니다. 이 책에서는 학습자가 평가의 주체가 되어 봄으로서 새로운 시각으로 본인의 글을 볼 수 있는 기회를 제공합니다. 학습자들은 **친숙한 한국문화를** 밑바탕으로 낯선 컨텐츠에 방해받지 않고 쓰기학습이라는 **본연의 목적에 충실**할 수 있도록 설계되었습니다.

저는 **진정한 영어 글쓰기를 위한 쓰기교육**을 학생들이 이 책과 함께 이루어 나가길 소망합니다. 학생들이 이 책에 빠져들며 영어 글쓰기 실력을 향상시키고 진정한 학습의 기쁨을 맛볼 수 있기를 진심으로 바랍니다.

이 책이 만들어지기까지 항상 용기를 주었던 나의 가족들, 학교 동기 선생님들, 교수님들, 친구들 그리고 나의 학생들과 학부형님 모두에게 감사 인사를 드리고 싶습니다.

나의 고민을 함께해주며 같이 울고 웃어준 나의 남편, 전화한통도 조심스러웠던 양가 부모님과 표지 제작에 많은 도움을 준 내 동생, 항상 용기를 주시고 나의 가치를 인정해 주셨던 성희선생님과 지선선생님, 그리고 소중한 오랜 인연 해정님, 멋진 코믹을 사용할 수 있게 기회를 열어 주신 PIXTON, 지금의 책이 있을 수 있게 열정적인 조언을 주셨던 정은영 교수님과 박혜옥 교수님, 그리고 누구보다 나의 발전에 불을 지피고 영감을 주며 지켜봐 주신 Chris 교수님께 special thanks 를 드리고 싶습니다.

2

[Prologue]

In Korea, there are many high-quality English textbooks available. However, most of these books are not genuinely connected to the lives and culture of Korean students; they are filled with foreign contexts and cultures. It saddened me to see students unable to relate to the content of these textbooks, causing them to lose interest in learning English. This raised questions in my mind: "What if there were materials centered around Korean culture?" "What if textbooks were closely linked to students' daily lives?"

These "what ifs" planted the seed of the thought, "Perhaps I can make a small change." While I may not be able to change everything, I wanted to be the starting point for providing English learning materials that reflect Korean culture and are familiar and comforting to students.

The "Discover Writing Discover Korea" series is comprised of a total of 10 volumes. As clearly indicated by its title, this series is a book for English writing. These ten volumes offer English **writing skills specific to various genres while also providing aspects of grammar not covered in other books.** Through this series, **students can also conduct self-evaluation**. In typical classroom environments, students are usually on the receiving end of evaluations. They are often bound to scores, not fully understanding the meaning of the evaluations or the reasons behind their results. This book gives learners the opportunity to become the evaluators themselves, allowing them to see their writing from a new perspective. The series is designed so that learners can remain true to the fundamental goal of writing education without being hindered by unfamiliar content, **based on the familiar backdrop of Korean culture.**

I hope that students embark on a journey of true English writing education with these books. I sincerely wish for them to immerse themselves in these books, improve their English writing skills, and experience the true joy of learning.

I would like to express my gratitude to my family, schoolmates, teachers, friends, and all my students and fellow educators who have always supported me in the creation of this book.

To my husband, who shared my concerns and laughed and cried with me, to my cautious parents who were always just a phone call away, to my younger sister who provided invaluable assistance in designing the cover, to Seonghee and Jisun, who always encouraged me and recognized my worth; to my precious long-time friend, Hae-jung; to PIXTON for opening the opportunity to use amazing comics, to Professor Eun-young Jeong and Professor Hye-ok Park, who provided passionate advice and most importantly, to Professor Chris Douloff, who has been a source of inspiration, guidance, and unwavering support in my personal growth—special thanks to you all.

ORGANIZATION OF THE BOOK

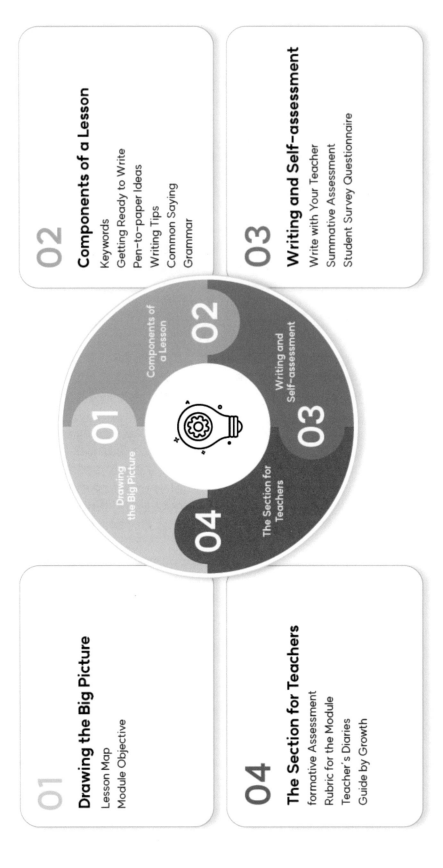

01 Drawing the Big Picture

Lesson Map
Module Objective

02 Components of a Lesson

Keywords
Getting Ready to Write
Pen-to-paper Ideas
Writing Tips
Common Saying
Grammar

03 Writing and Self-assessment

Write with Your Teacher
Summative Assessment
Student Survey Questionnaire

04 The Section for Teachers

formative Assessment
Rubric for the Module
Teacher's Diaries
Guide by Growth

Introduction of TLC, Genre Writing, and Process Writing

The teaching-learning cycle, genre writing, and process writing are three effective methods that interrelate and complement each other in fostering students' writing skills.

1. Teaching-Learning Cycle (TLC)

The Teaching-Learning Cycle is a systematic approach to teaching that involves four stages: **building the field** (contextualizing and building background knowledge), **modeling** (showcasing examples), **joint construction** (collaborative writing), and **independent construction** (students write on their own).

Relation to Other Methods: TLC acts as a framework where genre writing and process writing can be incorporated. For example, while modeling, you can introduce different genres and engage students in the process of writing stages.

Application: Start by engaging students with images or discussions to build context (**Building the Field**). Then, provide a well-structured example text (**Modelling**), followed by collaborative writing (**Joint Construction**). Finally, allow students to write independently.

2. Genre Writing

Genre writing focuses on teaching students about different text types or genres such as narratives, reports, or persuasive texts, and **the language features and structures commonly used** in each.

Relation to Other Methods: Within the TLC, different genres can be modeled and practiced. Process writing can be applied within a specific genre to go through the drafting, revising, and editing stages.

Application: Choose a **genre** and **model a text**, discussing its **specific language features** and **structures**. Then, **guide** students to write their own texts following the conventions of the chosen genre.

3. Process Writing

Process writing emphasizes the steps or processes in writing such as planning, drafting, revising, editing, and publishing.

Relation to Other Methods: It can be embedded within the TLC during the independent construction phase and can be utilized across different genres.

Application: Guide students through each stage, from brainstorming ideas (**Planning**), writing a first draft (**Drafting**), getting and giving feedback (**Revising**), correcting errors (**Editing**), to finally publishing their work.

The integration of these three methods offers a **comprehensive, structured, and student-centered approach to teaching writing**, which supports students in becoming autonomous, reflective, and proficient writers.

TABLE OF CONTENTS

LESSON MAP

MODULE 7: ADVERTISEMENT WRITING						
		GET READY TO WRITE			WRITE	REVISE & EDIT
KEYWORDS	MODEL TEXTS	PEN-TO-PAPER IDEAS & WRITING TIPS	GRAMMAR	WRITE WITH YOUR TEACHER	WRITE BY YOURSELF	EDITING
charming, floor-to-ceiling window, offer, charge, modern, breeze, by, book, pick-up service, shine	**We're Looking Forward to Your Message.**	• organize the text by the direction of the gaze. • explain details of the place • Common Saying: *looking forward to -*	• action verb + ing • fronting sentences	• completing the unfinished part of an advertisement	• challenge: write an advertisement under the given prompts	• check hyphen

Example Lesson Plans: Module 1 [8 classes, 6 hours]

Module objectives ⭐ **2**	*By the end of* **Module 1**, *a student will be better able to*
	O1. compose a self-introduction using simple, short sentences, and a first-person perspective considering the readership and purpose of the text.
	O2. understand language in chunks and fixed expressions
	O3. share personal information safely and appropriately, and use the appropriate tone.
	O4. apply simple vocabulary and present tense
	O5. understand the rules of the S-V agreement and apply them in writing.
Legend	TLC = Teaching learning cycle
Class 1	TLC stage: *Modelling*
Major Stages	**1.** Explain module objectives to S
	2. "Task A" (1–5): Have S read questions and discuss.
	3. "KEYWORDS": Have S check the target words and elicit their meaning. Help S pronounce words correctly. If needed, use **MORE EXERCISE FOR KEYWORDS**
	4. "Model Text": Have S read the given cartoon and understand the context. Give S a "Model Text" and encourage S to notice the target words in the text. Have S understand the content of the text using concept-checking questions (CCQ).
HW	**"HOMEWORK DAY 1"**
Class 2	TLC stage: *Modelling*
Major Stages	1. 1. **"HOMEWORK DAY 1":** to check + **"KEYWORDS":** to review + **"Model Text":** to review
	"**WRITING STRATEGIES**—"**Writing Process**": Have S read and discuss.
	1. **"DEEP DIVE":** Have S analyze **"Model Text"**. Have S consider the structure. S applies to **"DEEP DIVE A & B"**. If a learner doesn't have a partner, the teacher fills that role as a guide. Don't forget that the teacher's role is not only to teach but also to observe, and guide
HW	**"HOMEWORK DAY 2"**

Class 3	TLC stage: *Modelling*
Major Stages	1. **"HOMEWORK DAY 2"**: to check + **"KEYWORDS"**: to review + **"Model Text"**: to review
	2. **KEY ELEMENT & TIPS**—"**Self-introduction Etiquette"(Tip 1–6):** to check S understands tips for writing self-introduction. Have S complete **"EXERCISE 1, 2"**, **"HANDS-ON ACTIVITIES A, B"**, and **"DEEP DIVE A, B"**.
	3. **"SUMMARY"**: to review a letter-writing process
HW	**"HOMEWORK DAY 3"**
Class 4	TLC stage: *Modelling*
Major Stages	1. **"HOMEWORK DAY 3"**: to check + **"KEYWORDS"**: to review + **"Model Text"**: to review + **"Self-introduction Etiquette"(Tip1-6)**: to review
	2. **KEY ELEMENT & TIPS** —**Fixed Expression**: Have S read examples and elicit the expression's meaning. Have S solve **"EXERCISE 3–5"**.
	3. **"DEEP DIVE"**: Have S read **"Model Text"** and analyze the fixed expression in the text.
HW	**"HOMEWORK DAY 3"**
Class 5	TLC stage: *Modelling*
Major Stages	1. **"GRAMMAR 1"**: Have S think about when to use the present tense. Have S read **"GRAMMAR 1"** and provide some time to notice the function of the present tense. Have S solve **"EXERCISE 6"**. Conduct **CCQ.**
	2. **"DEEP DIVE A-D"**: Have S read "Model Text" and analyze.
	3. **"HANDS-ON ACTIVITIES A, B:** Have S solve.
HW	**"HOMEWORK DAY 5"**
Class 6	TLC stage: *Modelling*
Major Stages	1. "**HOMEWORK DAY 5**": to check + **"KEYWORDS"**: to review + **"Model Text"**: to review + **Self-introduction Etiquette (Tip1-6)** to review + **"Fixed Expression"**: to review + **"GRAMMAR 1"**: to review
	2. **"GRAMMAR 2-1"**: Have S think about the rule of present Be-verb. Have S read **"GRAMMAR 2-1"**. Have S solve **"EXERCISE 7"**. **Conduct CCQ.**
	2. **"GRAMMAR 2-2"**: Have S think about the rule of present Action-verb. Have S read **"GRAMMAR 2-2"**. Have S solve **"EXERCISE 8"**. **Conduct CCQ.**

	3. **"HANDS-ON ACTIVITIES"**: S makes sentences in "HANDS-ON ACTIVITIES A, B".
HW	**"HOMEWORK DAY 6"**
Class 7	TLC stage: *joint construction1–2*
Major Stages	1. **"HOMEWORK DAY 6"**: to check + **"KEYWORDS"**: to review + **"Model Text"**: to review + **Self-introduction Etiquette (Tip1-6)** to review + **"Fixed Expression"**: to review + **"GRAMMAR 1"**: to review "**GRAMMAR 1**": to review +"**GRAMMAR 2-1, 2-2"**: to review
	2. **"WRITE WITH YOUR TEACHER 1"**: Have S understand the purpose of the task. Guide S to complete the unfinished text. Demonstrate S how to revise and edit using the checklist.
	3. **"WRITE WITH YOUR TEACHER 2"**: Have S understand the task's purpose and demonstrate the process writing procedure. Complete the task with S.
HW	**"HOMEWORK DAY 7"**
Class 8	TLC stage: *Independent construction*
Major Stages	1. **"HOMEWORK DAY 7"**: to check + **"KEYWORDS"**: to review + **"Model Text"**: to review + **Self-introduction Etiquette (Tip1-6)** to review + **"Fixed Expression"**: to review + **"GRAMMAR 1"**: to review "**GRAMMAR 1**": to review +"**GRAMMAR 2-1, 2-2"**: to review + **"WRITE WITH YOUR TEACHER 2"**: to review the procedure of process writing
	2. **"INDEPENDENT WRITING"**: Have S understand the purpose of the task. Have S look through and complete the task.

MODULE OBJECTIVES

In this module, you will learn how to

- organize the text by direction of gaze.

- explain details of the place

- apply how to cohesively connect sentences using fronting style

- understand the procedures of pre-writing, drafting, revising, and editing

A.   Answer the questions. Discuss with your partner.
1. Do you have a cellphone? How does it look?
2. Is it easy or difficult to describe things? Why?
3. When do people describe?
4. What do people describe for?

KEYWORDS

Match the words with pictures. Check the meanings and pronunciation with your teacher.

There is no extra _____ for adding cheese to your burger.

• charming

The restaurant _____ a special menu on weekends.

• shine

Can you _____ a table for dinner at the Italian restaurant?

• offer

A cool _____ blew through the trees, making the leaves dance.

• charge

Her _____ smile made everyone in the room feel welcome.

• modern

We bought a _____ TV that can connect to the internet.

• by

• breeze

• book

• pick-up service

• floor-to-ceiling window

MORE EXERCISE FOR KEYWORDS

Exercise 1. Check the meaning of each word above again. Put them with the word that takes the same role in each box together. Work with your partner. Follow an example.

e.g., apple, bus, cat...	e.g., pretty, soft, big...	e.g., eat, have, run...

Exercise 2. Check the pronunciation and stress of each word. Work with your partner. Follow an example.

●
floor

●
ceil▪ing

●
mod▪ern

● ●
Pick-up service

★ **4**

Exercise 3. Look up the words again. Can you guess what story is in the text? Discuss with your partner.

MORE EXERCISE FOR KEYWORDS

Exercise 4. Fill in the gap with the words below.

> charming, floor-to-ceiling window, offer, charge, modern, breeze, by, book, pick-up service, shine

1. The apartment has a large _____ in the living room, offering a great city view.

2. There is a small _____ for using the high-speed Wi-Fi in the house.

3. In the evening, you can feel a gentle _____ coming from the sea.

4. We provide a _____ from the airport.

5. You can _____ a room with us using the phone or our website.

6. The morning light will _____ into your room, waking you up naturally.

7. At our cafe, we _____ a variety of homemade cakes.

8. Our house is located _____ a quiet and beautiful park.

9. For tech lovers, our place has a _____ home theater system.

10. Our Airbnb is located in a _____ little town surrounded by nature.

11. The famous bakery is located just _____ the street from our house.

12. You can easily _____ your stay with us online.

13. The bedroom has a _____ that looks out onto the mountains

14. As part of our service, we _____ free Wi-Fi to all our guests

15. Enjoy the latest entertainment with our _____ smart TV.

MODULE 7   WHERE IS THE BEST PLACE TO STAY?   5

Sally's grandmother is planning to visit Jeju island before going back home. Now Sally and her grandmother are looking for a good place.

Comic made at Pixton.com

Title

The title of the advertisement should be catchy and give an idea about the place.

Ocean Breeze: Traditional Jeju Island Hideaway

Introduction
This is the first part where you say hello and start talking about the place.

Hello! Welcome to our charming traditional home on the beautiful Jeju Island. Get ready for an adventure by the ocean!

Description of the Place
You describe what the house or room looks like. Think of it as painting a picture with words. You can mention how many rooms there are, what colors the walls are, if there's a garden, etc.

Right when you walk in, you'll find our little kitchen. In the kitchen, there's everything you need to cook, like pots and a small table for eating. Simple but nice is our bathroom. It has everything you need to get clean and fresh. In front of the bathroom is a cozy bedroom. It has a floor-to-ceiling window. The most amazing part of our house is the ocean view. Waking up with blue water and the bright sun shining on it every morning will refresh you. Our house is like a small piece of Jeju's calm and happy world.

Amenities and Features
This is where you list the special things your place offers, like a swimming pool, Wi-Fi, or a game room. Think of these as the special powers of your place.

Plus, there's a bus stop just 5 minutes away, so you can easily explore around.

Location Details
You tell where the place is located and what's nearby.

We offer a special free pick-up service to make your travel easier. If you want, we can also provide a delicious breakfast for a small extra charge.

Rules or Guidelines
You tell what guests can or cannot do, like no smoking or pets allowed.

Our home is a traditional Jeju house. It's simple and not super modern, but it's full of charm. We kindly ask you to take care of our home as if it were your own.

Contact Information
You tell how they can reach you if they want to stay at your place. Give your address or phone number.

Reach out for our lovely Jeju home at oceanbreezejeju@islandhomes.com. You also contact us on Instagram @OceanBreezeJejuHome or +82 123 4567.

We're looking forward to your message and can't wait to welcome you to our Ocean Breeze home. we hope you'll love it as much as we do!

Closing
You can say something nice and inviting.

Comic made at Pixton.com

WHAT IS THE DIRECTION OF THE GAZE AND WHY IS IT IMPORTANT?

Comic made at Pixton.com

1. What is the Direction of Gaze?

The direction of gaze is like following your eyes as they move around a room or a place. Imagine your eyes are a camera, moving from one thing to the next. It helps you describe what you see in the order you see it.

2. Why is the Direction of Gaze Important?

▪ **Organized Description:** It helps to describe a place in an organized way, just like telling a story from the beginning to the end.

▪ **Easy to Understand:** When you describe things in the order you see them, it makes your description easy for others to understand and picture.

▪ **Complete Picture:** This method ensures you don't miss out on describing important parts of a place.

3. Why is the Direction of Gaze Used in AirBnB Advertisements?

In AirBnB advertisements, the direction of gaze is used because it's like giving a virtual tour. It helps people imagine the place as if they are walking through it, seeing everything in a logical and inviting way. It's like guiding them through the house, room by room, feature by feature.

4. What Kind of Direction Should We Follow?

You should follow a direction that feels natural, like how you would look around a room:

- Start at the entrance: Describe what you see when you first walk in.
- Move left to right: Just like reading a book, describe items from left to right.
- From top to bottom: Mention things up high like lights or paintings, then things lower like furniture.
- Front to back: Start with what's closest to you, then describe what's further away.

DEEP DIVE

A. Look at the model text. Then answer the questions.

1. What genre does the text belong to?

2. What is the purpose of the text?

3. How many parts are in the text? Can you explain the function of each part?

B. Look at the model text. Then answer the questions.

1. Who was the reader of the text?

2. Who was the writer?

3. How close is the reader and the writer? How do you know it?

4. Find the direction of the gaze from the model text.

C. Fill in the blanks with the body parts. Read the advertisement below and circle the writer and reader. Then underline the purpose of this text.

Halla Retreat: Cozy Mountain Home in Jeju

_____

Hello there! Welcome to our cozy home by the magnificent Hallasan in Jeju Island. Prepare for a mountain adventure!

When you step inside, you'll see our cute kitchen. Here, you have everything to cook your favorite meals, including pots and a small eating area. Our bathroom is simple and clean, perfect for a refreshing shower. Next to the bathroom is a comfortable bedroom with a big window from the floor-to-the ceiling. Through the window you can see Halla Mountain and its green forests every morning. It feels like a peaceful part of Jeju's nature is right in your home.

Plus, our house is super close to Hallasan, only a short walk away!

We offer a handy free pick-up service to help you get here without any trouble. And, if you're hungry in the evening, we can make you dinner for a little extra.

Our home is traditional Jeju-style. It's not very modern, but it's cozy and full of character. We ask you to please take care of it as if it were your own.

To book your stay in our lovely Jeju mountain home, just send us a message at hallasanretreat@mountainhomes.com. You also contact us on Instagram @HallasanRetreatJeju and +82 234 5678

We can't wait to hear from you and welcome you to our wonderful home by the mountain!

Comic made at Pixton.com

TIP 1   **TITLE**

Choose a short and catchy title that gives an idea of what your place is like. A good title grabs attention and makes people want to read more. Use words that describe your place's best feature, like "Cozy," "Sunny," "Beachfront," etc.

e.g., Cozy Beachfront Cottage
e.g., Mountain View Apartment.

EXERCISE 1. Read situation. Write appropriate titles for each situation. Follow the example.

e.g., Our little cottage sits right by the sea, with a warm and comfy room that's perfect for relaxing. You can hear the waves and feel the sea breeze from every corner of the house.

→ Cozy Beachfront Cottage

Situation 1. Right in the heart of downtown, our place is close to shops and cafes. It's small but very convenient for exploring the city

→ _____

Situation 2. Our house has a big garden with lots of flowers and a small pond. It's a perfect place to play outside and enjoy sunny days.

→ _____

Situation 3. This apartment is high up in the city, where you can see all the lights at night. It's modern and bright, with big windows to enjoy the view.

→ _____

TIP2   INTRODUCTION

Start with a friendly greeting and a brief introduction to your place. It makes readers feel welcome and eager to learn more. Use words that make your place sound inviting, like "Welcome," "Discover," "Escape," etc.

e.g., Welcome to our sunny beachfront home!
e.g., Hi! Come and see our cozy cabin in the middle of the forest. It's perfect for a quiet and peaceful time.

EXERCISE 2. Read the titles above. Write an appropriate introduction for each title. Follow the example.

e.g., Title: Sunny beachfront home.
          Introduction: Welcome to our sunny beachfront home!

1.
Title:_____

Introduction:_____

2.
Title:_____

Introduction:_____

3.
Title:_____

Introduction:_____

DESCRIPTION OF THE PLACE

Describe what your place looks like, including rooms, decor, and any unique features. This helps guests imagine themselves in your place. Be clear and descriptive. Use simple sentences to describe each part of your place.

EXERCISE 3. Look at the pictures. Imagine each picture is your place and describe what the place looks like.

Picture	Description of the place
e.g.,	**e.g.,** In our home, the living room is a special place. It's big and bright, with big windows. Through the windows you can see the forest. There are comfy sofas to relax on and lots of space to play games or watch TV.

TIP4 **LOCATION DETAILS**

Explain where your place is and what's nearby, like attractions or transportation. Guests want to know what they can do around your place and how easy it is to get there. **Mention landmarks, tourist spots, or convenient transport options.**

e.g., Surrounded by nature trails, our cabin is a 10-minute walk from the lake and a short drive from local shops.

EXERCISE 4. Look at the pictures. Imagine what guests can do around your place. Write activities for each picture.

Picture	Location Details
e.g.,	**e.g.,** Surrounded by nature trails, our cabin is a 10-minute walk from the lake and a short drive from local shops.

MORE EXERCISE FOR LOCATION DETAILS

EXERCISE 1. Look at the picture. Write the location details of each picture considering TIP 4.

Picture	Location Details

AMENITIES AND FEATURES

List the special things your place offers, like Wi-Fi, a garden, or a swimming pool. These details can make your place more appealing. Think about what makes your place special or comfortable and highlight those things.

e.g., We offer a hot tub, a selection of board games, and a beautiful garden to explore.

EXERCISE 5. Look at the pictures. Write what you can offer to your guests when they stay at your place.

Picture	Amenities and Features
e.g., 	e.g., Enjoy a lovely patio with a barbecue grill.

TIP6   HOUSE RULES

Clearly state any rules guests should follow, like no smoking or specific check-in times. This helps avoid any misunderstandings later. Make sure they're simple, polite and easy to understand.

e.g., Please no smoking inside the house and respect the quiet hours after 10 PM.
e.g., We love pets, but our cabin isn't suitable for them. Also, please take off your shoes inside.

EXERCISE 6. Make house rules that you think guests need to keep while staying in your place.

1.

_____

2.

_____

3.

_____

TIP7   CONTACT INFORMATION

Provide details on how guests can contact you or book your place. Guests need a way to reach out to you for more information or to make a reservation. Include an email, phone number, or social media link. Make sure the information is correct and easy to find.

e.g., To book your beach holiday, email us at sunnybeachgetaway@islandmail.com or call us at +123 456 7890.

e.g., Reach out for a magical forest experience at tranquilcabin@forestmail.com or contact us on Instagram @TranquilForestCabin.

EXERCISE 7. Make the contact information to help the guest to reach out.

1.

_____

2.

_____

3.

_____

TIP8   **CLOSING**

End with a friendly and inviting message, encouraging guests to book your place. Use phrases like **"We can't wait to welcome you"** or **"Looking forward to hosting you."**

e.g., We're excited to host you to our beachside home!
e.g., We can't wait to welcome you to our cabin.

EXERCISE 8. Make the closing to help the guest reach out.

1.
_____

2.
_____

3.
_____

DEEP DIVE

A. Read the Airbnb advertisement below. Compare it with the Model Text. Then find seven mistakes and correct them. Work with your partner.

Hi! We welcome you to our modern and stylish home close to the famous Seongsan Ilchulbong on Jeju Island. Get ready for a fun time near the sea and beautiful nature!

Our home is bright and new with cool, modern designs. When you come in, you'll see a big living room with comfy sofas and a TV. The kitchen has everything you need like a fridge and a microwave. The bathroom is clean and shiny, and the bedroom has a big, cozy bed. Every room has large windows, so the house is always full of sunlight.

Our house is near the amazing Seongsan Ilchulbong, where you can see the sunrise over the ocean. It's really easy to get here by bus from Jeju Airport, so no worries about travel!

We don't have a free pick-up service.

Please be careful and treat our home like your own. And remember, no pets or smoking inside.

We think you'll have a great time here, enjoying both comfort and adventure!

To book your modern stay near Seongsan Ilchulbong, please send us a message.

B. Read the Model Text. Underline **Tip1–6** in the text.

AIRBNB ADVERTISEMENT

An Airbnb Advertisement writing process: (1) **Write a catchy title** that tells what your Airbnb is like. (2) **Write a Short Introduction** to tell why your Airbnb is a great place to stay. (3) **Write about what your Airbnb looks like inside** such as rooms and the decoration. (4) **Explain where your Airbnb is** and what is close by, like parks or shops. (5) **Write down what guests can use at your Airbnb**, like Wi-Fi or a swimming pool. (6) Clearly **say what guests can do and what they should not do** at your Airbnb. (7) **Write a nice sentence** to tell guests you would like them to come and stay. (8) **Tell guests how they can contact you or book your Airbnb** Including an email or phone number.

Title

Introduction

Description of the place

Location details

Amenities and features

House rules

Contact information

Closing

These tips are helpful when you describe rooms and places, making a picture in readers' minds. It's real English for real situations that are fun and creative.

Comic made at Pixton.com

I **_am looking forward to_** our family trip to the beach this summer.
We **_are looking forward to_** the new superhero movie.

People use **_looking forward to-_** when they are excited about something that is going to happen. It's like when people can't wait for something fun or good in the future. **_Looking forward to-_** is placed **before the Be-verb verb** (e.g., be, is, was, etc.) in a sentence. **Nouns** are placed **after _looking forward to-_.**

Whenever you feel happy and excited about something that will happen later, like a trip, a holiday, or even seeing a friend, you can say **_I am looking forward to it._** It's a way to express your happiness about the future.

EXERCISE 9. Read the given situations. Write your own sentences with **_looking forward to-._** Follow the example.

Situation

e.g., Your birthday is coming soon. You are happy and excited about your party. What will you say?

e.g., I am looking forward to my birthday party.

1. There's a new park opening near the school. Mi-young is very excited and curious about it. What will she say?

→ _____

2. For an upcoming school trip, there is an arranged pick-up service from the airport. Gun-woo is very excited and happy about it. What will he say?

→ _____

3. After buying a new camera online, Se-yoon is very excited and wants to see it as soon as possible. What will he say?

→ _____

EXERCISE 10. Write your own sentences using *looking forward to-...*.

1._____

2._____

3._____

4._____

DEEP DIVE

A. Read the Model Text again. Why did the writer say *looking forward to-...*? Discuss with your partner.

ACTION VERB + ING

Comic made at Pixton.com

- Functioning as a **noun**:

e.g., **Jogging** is a good exercise."
e.g., I enjoy **reading**.
e.g., Sally is looking forward to **visiting** her grandmother.

- Working to **tell something is happening right now**
e.g., Ji-hyun **is running** a marathon.

- Working as **an adjective**
e.g., **The girl running to the park** is Ji-hyun.

When you add **-ing** to an action verb, its function in sentences can vary.

EXERCISE 11. Read the sentences. Match the function of **_action verb+ing_**. Work with your partner.

Using the pick-up service makes traveling easier.   ·

I am booking tickets online.   ·   · Functioning as a **noun**

A gentle breeze blowing through the trees is cool.   ·

The sunshine is brightening the room.   ·   · Working to **tell something is happening right now**

Charging a fee for extra services is common in hotels.   ·

Her charming smile makes everyone feel welcome.   ·   · Working as **an adjective**

Having floor-to-ceiling windows makes the room brighter.   ·

EXERCISE 12. Look at the picture and make sentences with *action verb + ing*.

1.		e.g., (walk) The man <u>walking</u> to the postbox is the king. The king <u>is walking</u> to the post box. <u>Walking</u> to the postbox is not difficult for the king.
2.		(feed) The man _____ the chickens is the king. The king _____ the chickens. _____ the chickens is an easy job.
3.		(fight) The monster _____ the king is a huge grey squid. The monster _____ the king. _____ the monster is not easy to the king.
4.		(swim) The man _____ in space is the king. The king _____ in space. _____ in the space is amazing.
5.		(see) The man _____ the moon is the king. The king _____ the moon. _____ the moon at night is romantic.

Comic made at Pixton.com

EXERCISE 13. Read the Model text. Find *action + ing*. Group them in the box below. Think why the writer uses *action + ing* in the sentences. Work with your partner.

Functioning as a noun	Working to tell something is happening right now	Working as an adjective

EXERCISE 14. Read the sentences. Combine two sentences into one.

e.g., The man is fighting the monster. He is the king. → The man fighting the monster is the king.

e.g., The king is fighting the monster. It is not fun to the king. → Fighting the monster is not fun for the king.

1. The boy is eating bibimbab. He is Jin-ha.

   → _____

2. Hae-jin is playing a computer game named Zelda. It is Hae-jin's hobby.

   → _____

3. Dan-hee is swimming in the sea. It is not difficult for Dan-hee.

   → _____

4. The boys are my friends. They are playing soccer.

   → _____

DEEP DIVE

A. When we see *action + ing* itself, is it possible to guess the meaning of *action + ing*? Discuss with your partner.

MORE EXERCISE FOR GRAMMAR1

Exercise 1. Read the sentences. Match the function of *action verb+ing*.

I am reading a fascinating book
about dinosaurs   ·

Swimming is my favorite sport.   ·   · **Functioning as a noun**

A bright sun shining in the sky is
warm.   ·

A quiet bird singing in the morning is ·
beautiful.

They are swimming in the pool on ·
this hot day

The laughing children played in the ·   · **Working to tell something is**
park.   **happening right now**

He is playing soccer with his friends ·
in the park.

She wore a shining necklace to the
party.   ·

Jogging in the park is a great way to ·
start the day.

They saw a flying bird above the
trees.   ·

He found a glowing firefly in the ·   · **Working as an adjective**
garden at night.

Reading helps you learn new things. ·

37

Exercise 2. Change the given sentence. Follow the example.

e.g., He found a glowing firefly in the garden at night. → He found a firefly glowing in the garden at night.
e.g., We watched a peacock dancing in the zoo. → We watched a dancing peacock in the zoo.

1. She saw a singing bird on the tree. →

→ _____

2. She saw a cat sleeping on the sofa. →

→ _____

3. They heard a dog barking outside. →

→ _____

4. He caught a jumping frog in the backyard. →

→ _____

Exercise 3. Look at the pictures. Write What the king is doing. Follow the example.

e.g.,	(see) e.g., The king is seeing the whale's tail.
	(sit) →
	→

Comic made at Pixton.com

Exercise 4. Compare the meaning of each sentence in Exercise 2-3. Do they have the same or different meanings?

When we write or speak, sometimes we want to make our sentences more interesting or focus on a certain part of the sentence. This is where 'fronting' comes in handy.

'Fronting' means putting a part of a sentence at the beginning, even though it's not usually found there.

Comic made at Pixton.com

e.g., A cat was sitting on the mat. → Sitting on the mat was a cat.

This makes our sentence sound more interesting and can draw attention to the cat and what it's doing. People use this style in writing (and speaking) to:

1. **Make sentences more exciting or different**: Sometimes, sentences can sound more fun or grab the reader's attention better when they start in an unusual way.

2. **Emphasize something special**: If there's a part of the sentence that is really important, like the action or how something is done, putting that part at the beginning can make it stand out more.

3. **Tell stories or describe scenes**: Writers often use fronting to paint a picture in the reader's mind, making the scene or action feel more alive.

4. **Cohesion:** When we use fronting, we often link the sentence to something we said before. This means our sentences connect well with each other.

EXERCISE 15. Read the sentences. Change them into fronting style. Follow the example.

e.g., The wind was blowing through the trees. → Blowing through the trees was the wind.

1. The stars were shining at night. →

2. A fish was swimming in the pond. →

3. The sun was setting behind the mountains. →

More exercise for Grammar2

EXERCISE 1. Read the sentences. Change them into fronting style. Follow the example.

1. A dog is barking loudly.

2. The leaves are falling from the tree.

3. A baby is crying in the room.

4. The train is moving fast on the tracks.

5. A teacher is reading a book.

6. A boat is sailing on the lake.

7. A cup is in the cupboard.

8. Colorful cushions are on the sofa.

9. A little kitchen is next to the bedroom.

10. A beautiful painting is hanging on the wall.

EXERCISE 2. Look at the pictures. Write where the king is in the fronting style.

e.g.,	e.g., In the bedroom is the king.
	Comic made at Pixton.com

DEEP DIVE

A. Do you see fronting sentences often? Discuss with your partner.

B. Why are *fronting sentences* used in the Model text? What is the advantage of using *them*? Discuss with your partner.

HANDS-ON ACTIVITIES

A. Look at the picture. Describe the picture. Follow the example.

	e.g., There are big windows. Through the windows sunshine comes. Next to the window is a tall mirror. It has a black frame. In front of the mirror is a plant pot. Next to them is a cozy and big bed.
	_____ _____
	_____ _____

B. Write your own fronting style sentences. Work with your partner.

1._____

2._____

3._____

You are writing an Airbnb advertisement in Jeju. The advertisement should include:

• title

• introduction

• details and features of the place

• house rules

• closing and contact information

• use *looking forward to* appropriately.

• use fronting sentence style appropriately.

GAPS

Genre:		Purpose:	
Audience:		Style:	

WRITE

_____ _____ _____ _____ _____ _____	**Discover the Tangerine Dream House in Jeju!** Hello Friends! Welcome to our very special home in Jeju, where tangerines grow and stars shine bright at night! Our home is really cool! It looks just like the houses in Jeju from a long time ago. When you come in, you'll see a little garden. On the left side of the garden is the kitchen where everyone can cook and eat together. It's fun to share! _____ the house, you can see the floors called Daecheongmaru. It is a wooden porch that connects all rooms in the house. It's a fun place to play! _____ are bedrooms. They have big windows from _____, so you can see outside. Here's something really exciting. _____ our house is a tangerine farm. You can pick tangerines! They are juicy and sweet. And at night, we'll take you to Byeolbit Oreum to see the stars. They _____ tiny lights in the sky! Please treat our home with care, just like your own. Let's keep it quiet after 10 PM so everyone can have a peaceful sleep. Remember to turn off lights and taps when not in use. Our home is simple, not like the _____ buildings in the city. But it's full of fun and charm. We all share the kitchen and bathroom, which makes it feel like a big family. We can _____ when you arrive! _____ for breakfast, but it's really yummy. Want to come and stay? Here's how you can _____:

	- Email us: tangerinefarmjeju@rusticretreats.com - Call us: +82 234 5678 - Or message us on Instagram: @TangerineFarmJejuStay We are _____ at our Tangerine Dream House. You're going to love it!

CHECKLIST

• Did I organize the text in an Airbnb advertisement style? _____

• Did I consider the direction of the gaze? _____

• Did I use fronting style sentences appropriately? _____

• Did I mention details and features of the place with adjectives to attract visitors? _____

• Did I use *looking forward to…*? _____

• Did I make a title keeping rules? _____

• Did I understand the procedures of pre-writing, drafting, revising, and editing? _____

WRITE WITH YOUR TEACHER 2	The purpose of this task is for you to practice advertisement writing.

You are an owner of one place in Jeju. Now you are writing an Airbnb advertisement. The advertisement should include:

• title

• introduction

• details and features of the place

• house rules

• closing and contact information

• use *looking forward to* appropriately.

• use fronting sentence style appropriately.

GAPS

Genre:		Audience:	
Purpose:		Style:	

PREWRITING

DRAFT

FINAL DRAFT

CHECKLIST

• Did I organize the text in an Airbnb advertisement style? _____

• Did I consider the direction of the gaze? _____

• Did I use fronting style sentences appropriately? _____

• Did I mention details and features of the place with adjectives to attract visitors? _____

• Did I use *looking forward to...*? _____

• Did I make a title keeping rules? _____

• Did I understand the procedures of pre-writing, drafting, revising, and editing? _____

Formative Assessment: HOMEWORK

HOMEWORK DAY 1	KEYWORDS

1. Fill in the blanks with the words in the box below. You might need to change the form of the words (*e.g., play > playing, plays, or played*). The words might be used more than once or they might not be used at all.

---

charming, floor-to-ceiling window, offer, charge, modern, breeze, by, book, pick-up service, shine

---

Your Fun Stay at the Saryeoni Supgil Home!

Welcome young friends! Get ready for a super fun time at our house ___ the Saryeoni Supgil in Jeju!

Right when you walk in, you'll see our big kitchen. It's a place where everyone can cook together. It's bright and has all you need to make yummy food!

Next to the kitchen, you'll find our living room. It's a cool spot to hang out with _____ windows. These windows let you see the beautiful outside and let the sunshine in! Around the living room, there are four bedrooms. Each one is _____ and has its own bathroom. So, you have your own private space!

Our house is modern, which means it has fast Wi-Fi and comfortable places to sit. You can chill, chat with friends, or plan your next day's adventure. Remember, we _____ a cool night-time photo service! For a small _____, you can take amazing photos under the stars. It's super fun and a great way to remember your trip.

We don't have _____, but there's a bus stop only 7 minutes away by walking. So, you can easily come and explore all the cool things in Jeju.

Please treat our home with care, just like your own. To keep the house comfortable for everyone, we can't allow pets.

Ready to _____ your adventure? Just contact us:
- Email: sarabongforesthouse@jejuadventures.com
- Call: +82 345 6789
- Message on Instagram: @SarabongForestHouse

We are looking forward to seeing you at our home. It's going to be awesome!

1. Fill in the blanks with the words in the box below. You might need to change the form of the words (*e.g., play > playing, plays, or played*). The words might be used more than once or they might not be used at all.

> charming, floor-to-ceiling window, offer, charge, modern, breeze, by, book, pick-up service, shine

Your Magical Stay at the Hydrangea Garden Home!

Hello, young ladies! Are you ready for a girls-only adventure at our home Hydrangea Garden in Jeju?

As soon as you enter, you'll be greeted by our Hydrangea Garden. It's a _____ and colorful space where everyone can take pictures. You might get a memorable photograph. When you step into the house, you will see the bright and cheerful kitchen where everyone can cook together. Imagine making tasty treats surrounded by the scent of flowers! Next to the kitchen is our living room with

_____

These windows offer a stunning view of the garden and let the sun's rays dance inside! It's a perfect spot to relax and admire the beautiful hydrangeas. Around the living room are three bedrooms, each _____ and equipped with its own bathroom. You'll have your private cozy corner to rest and dream!

At night, we _____ a fantastic BBQ party! For a small _____, join all the girls in the dormitory for a night of delicious food and laughter under the stars.

While we don't have a_____, our home is just 30 minutes from Jeju Airport by bus. It's super easy to find us!

Please treat our home with care, just like your own. Remember to turn off lights and taps when not in use.

Are you excited to _____ your stay? Just reach out to us:
- Email: hydrangeagardenhome@jejuadventures.com
- Call: +82 456 7890
- Instagram Message: @HydrangeaGardenHome

We are looking forward to welcoming you to our Hydrangea Garden Home. It's going to be a wonderful time filled with flowers, fun, and friendships!

2. Write about the direction of the gaze and its importance.

3. Read the text above again. Follow the direction of the gaze in the text.

_____ → _____ → _____ → _____ → _____

4. Read and the text above. Find the GAPS of the given text. Then complete the table below.

Genre:	Audience:
Purpose:	Style:

HOMEWORK DAY 3	EFFECTIVE INSTRUCTION TIPS

1. Fill in the blanks with the words in the box below. You might need to change the form of the words (*e.g., play > playing, plays, or played*). The words might be used more than once or they might not be used at all.

charming, floor-to-ceiling window, offer, charge, modern, breeze, by, book, pick-up service, shine

Your Cozy Getaway at the Yongduam Rock Home!

Hello, young sea explorers! Are you ready for an exciting stay near the Yongduam Rock in Jeju? Our cozy house is just perfect for you!

As soon as you enter, you'll find a small but well-equipped kitchen. It's perfect for making snacks or a quick meal. It's bright and has everything you need to cook up something tasty!

Next to the kitchen is our small living room. It has a big _____ that lets you see the beautiful sea and feel the refreshing sea _____. The sunlight _____ through makes it a happy place to chill!

house has one bedroom that's super cozy and _____. It's just right for two people and comes with its own small bathroom. If you want to bring a friend along, no problem! For a small extra _____, we can provide an extra set of blankets and a pillow. But remember, three people is the max in the room.

We _____ a cool service where you can rent bicycles to explore around! It's a fun way to see the sights and enjoy the sea air.

We don't have a _____, but don't worry. You can get here from Jeju Airport in just 20 minutes by bus. And, we have lots of space for parking if you come by car.

Please treat our home with care, just like your own. Let's keep it quiet after 10 PM so everyone can have a peaceful sleep.

Ready to _____ your fun trip? Just reach out to us:
- Email: yongduamrockhome@jejuadventures.com
- Call: +82 456 7890
- Instagram: @YongduamRockHome

We are so excited to welcome you to our charming little house by the sea. It's going to be a wonderful time!

2. Write about the structure of the Airbnb-style advertisement.

3. Read and circle the mistakes. Then correct them. If needed, you can research.

Your Awesome Family Getaway at Kwakji Beach Home!

Hey there, cool kids and families! Are you ready for an amazing stay at our house near Kwakji Beach in Jeju? Let's find out what makes our place so special!

Our house has two bedrooms. The master room is perfect for parents, and the second room is great for kids. Both are cozy and come with a big bathroom. Plus, every room has a great view!

our living area is next to the kitchen, with big floor-to-ceiling windows. It's a great place for family time or relaxing with a book. You can see the beautiful scenery and feel the sea breeze while chilling out.

As soon as you enter, you'll be greeted by our large, modern kitchen. It's perfect for cooking family meals, with lots of light and all the tools you need.

We offer a cool parasol rental service for the beach. You can relax in the shade and enjoy the soft white sand made of coral. It's perfect for a sunny day by the sea!

While we don't have a pick-up service, don't worry! Our place has a spacious parking lot, so bringing your family car is easy.

Just a short walk away, you'll find lots of cafes and restaurants by the beach. Sip on cool drinks and enjoy the stunning view of the emerald sea.

We can't wait to see you and your family at our charming Kwakji Beach Home.

Ready to book your family adventure? Just reach out to us:
- Email: kwakjibeachhome@jejuadventures.com
- Call: +82 456 7890
- Message on Instagram: @KwakjiBeachHome

Please treat our home with care, just like your own. To keep the house comfortable for everyone, we can't allow pets.

1. Fill in the blanks with the words in the box below. You might need to change the form of the words (*e.g., play > playing, plays, or played*). The words might be used more than once or they might not be used at all.

charming, floor-to-ceiling window, offer, charge, modern, breeze, by, book, pick-up service, shine, looking forward to

Your Cool Beachside Stay at Samyang Beach Home!

Hello, young beach lovers! Are you ready for an exciting stay at our place near Samyang Beach in Jeju?

When you walk in, you'll find a cozy kitchen, perfect for making snacks or small meals. It's small but has everything you need!

Next to the kitchen is our living space. It may be a bit old, but it's full of _____. It has comfortable seating and _____ that let you see the beautiful beach and feel the cool sea _____. At the corner of the living area is one room. It's simple and comfortable, with a small bathroom all to yourself.

Samyang Beach is unique because it's made of basalt, giving it cool black sand. It's a special place you'll love exploring!

Our home is in a small, peaceful town _____ the beach. You can see how local people live and enjoy a quiet, relaxing time.

We _____ a special breakfast service—delicious abalone porridge—that our Airbnb is famous for! It's a tasty way to start your day. Remember, there's a _____ for this service.

We provide _____, so getting to our place is super easy and stress-free.

Please treat our home with care, just like your own. Let's keep it quiet after 10 PM so everyone can have a peaceful sleep.

Ready to _____ your beach adventure? Just contact us:
- Email: samyangbeachhome@jejuadventures.com
- Call: +82 567 8901
- Message on Instagram: @SamyangBeachHome

We are _____ hosting you to our Samyang Beach Home. It's going to be an unforgettable stay _____ the sea!

2. When can we use *looking forward to* -.? Give one example that the expression can be used.

3. Fill in the blanks and complete sentences.

Situation 1: Next week, you're going to a summer camp where you can learn to swim. You are very excited and can't wait for it. Write a sentence expressing your excitement.

_____.

Situation 2: Your class is going on a field trip to an amusement park next month. You are thrilled about the trip and can hardly wait.

_____.

Situation 3: Your family is planning a vacation to the beach this summer. You are overjoyed and can't wait to play in the sand. Share how you feel about this trip.

_____.

Situation 4: You have entered an art competition, and the results will be announced next week. You feel very happy and are eagerly awaiting the announcement.

_____.

Situation 5: You have enrolled in a cooking class to learn how to bake cookies. You're so excited about learning and can't wait for the class to start. Express your eagerness for the class.

_____.

HOMEWORK DAY 5	ACTION + ING

1. Fill in the blanks with the words in the box below. You might need to change the form of the words (*e.g., play > playing, plays, or played*). The words might be used more than once or they might not be used at all.

charming, floor-to-ceiling window, offer, charge, modern, breeze, by, book, pick-up service, shine, looking forward to

Your Family Adventure at Pyoseon Haevichi Beach House!

Hello, welcome to our Beachside Home! Ready for a super cool stay ____ Pyoseon Haevichi Beach in Jeju? Let's dive into what makes our beach house amazing!

As soon as you step inside, you'll find a bright and spacious kitchen. It's perfect for cooking up family meals or snacks before heading to the beach.

Next to the kitchen is the large living room with _____. Around the living area are two bedrooms. Each room has its own bathroom. comfortable are both rooms. They are just right for a family of four. The rooms are _____, with big windows to let the sunshine in and give you a glimpse of the sea. The beach is super close and the water is shallow, making it great for little kids to play safely. Imagine building sandcastles and splashing around without worry! You also will find natural tide pools on the beach. They're like mini aquariums where you can see small crabs and fish. It's like being a marine explorer!

Just a 5-minute walk away, there's a famous pork belly restaurant. And if you love seafood, there's a market nearby where you can buy fresh mackerel sashimi and peeled shrimp sashimi.

We don't _____ a _____, but our place is easy to find and there's lots of fun nearby.

Please treat our home with care, just like your own. To keep the house comfortable for everyone, we can't allow pets.

Ready to _____your family beach adventure? Contact us:
- Email: pyoseonbeachhouse@jejuadventures.com
- Call: +82 567 8901
- Instagram: @PyoseonBeachHouse

We're _____ seeing you at our charming Pyoseon Haevichi Beach House.

2. Write about the functions of *action + ing* in the sentences.

3. Look at the picture. Make phrases or sentences using *action+ing*. Follow the example.

Pictures	Sentence
e.g.,	(fly, happy) → The flying king → The king is flying. → The king flying at the airport is happy.
1.	(swim, scared) → → →
2.	(draw, upset) → → →
3. Comic made at Pixton.com	(teach, energetic) → → →

4. Read the sentences. Combine the sentences into one. Follow the examples.

e.g., I see the bird. + The bird is singing in the tree. → I see the bird singing in the tree.
e.g., The bird is singing. + The bird is sitting on the roof. → The singing bird is sitting on the roof.

1. You can see the sea. + The sea is shining.
→

2. The sea is shining. + The sea is beautiful in the morning.
→

3. You can see the start at the top of the hill. + The stars are glowing.
→

4. The stars are glowing. + The stars look like gems.
→

5. You can see the reef. + the reef is waving.
→

1. Fill in the blanks with the words in the box below. You might need to change the form of the words (*e.g., play > playing, plays, or played*). The words might be used more than once or they might not be used at all.

---

charming, floor-to-ceiling window, offer, charge, modern, breeze, by, book, pick-up service, shine, looking forward to-

---

Welcome to the Fun Iho Tewoo Beach House!

Hello! Are you excited to visit our cool traditional house near Iho Tewoo Beach in Jeju? Let's check out what makes our place so special!

Our house looks like the old houses in Jeju. It has a stone wall made of special rocks called basalt. When you come in, there's a small garden and a cute Korean-style porch. This porch connects two rooms and a kitchen in the middle. It's like the heart of our house! You'll have your own room with a warm floor called ondol. It's how many Korean houses stay warm. The walls are covered with a special Korean paper named Hanji. It's really neat! Both rooms don't have _____ but they are _____. Between the rooms is a well-equipped bathroom for everyone. The kitchen is also shared with everyone. It's a great place to meet other people and talk about your day at the beach.

The beach has these unique horse-shaped lighthouses that are red and white. They're super cool for taking pictures! Plus, there are places nearby to get fresh mango and orange juice. Yummy!

Just 3 minutes away by walking, there's a famous restaurant where they grill a fish called hairtail. It's really tasty and famous here!

We don't _____ a _____, but there's a bus stop only five minutes away on foot. So, it's easy to come and have fun!

Please treat our home with care, just like your own. Let's keep it quiet after 10 PM so everyone can have a peaceful sleep.

Want to come and stay? Here's how you can _____:
- Email: ihotewoobeachhouse@jejuadventures.com
- Call: +82 678 9012
- Instagram: @IhoTewooBeachHouse

We're _____ to seeing you at our Iho Tewoo Beach House. It's going to be so much fun!

2. Write about how and when to use *fronting sentences* with an example sentence.

3. Read the text. Change some sentences into fronting sentences to make the text have more cohesion.

Fun Times at Cheonjiyeon Waterfall House!

Hi! Are you excited to stay near the Cheonjiyeon Waterfall in Jeju? Let's check out our cool house!

Our house is modern and it's right next to a cliff. That means you can see the sea all the time!

When you come in, you'll find a living room with floor-to-ceiling windows. you can see the ocean and feel the cool sea breeze through these windows. There is also a small kitchen where you can make snacks and meals on the right side of the living room. It has everything you need. A bathroom is next to the bedroom. It is small but has everything you need. The bedroom is next to the bathroom. It's not big, but it's really nice. There's a cozy bed and a big window, so you can feel the fresh wind and see the sea when you wake up.

If you're cold and need more blankets or a pillow, just tell us.

Just a 5-minute walk away, there's a great restaurant that serves dishes in earthenware pots. You must try their yummy food! We don't offer a free pick-up service, but no worries! There's a bus from the airport that comes right to our place.

Please treat our home with care, just like your own. To keep the house comfortable for everyone, we can't allow pets.

Want to stay with us? Here's how to book:
- Email: cheonjiyeonhouse@jejuadventures.com
- Call: +82 789 0123
- Instagram: @CheonjiyeonWaterfallHouse

We can't wait to see you at our Cheonjiyeon Waterfall House!

1. Fill in the blanks with the words in the box below. You might need to change the form of the words (*e.g., play > playing, plays, or played*). The words might be used more than once or they might not be used at all.

> charming, floor-to-ceiling window, offer, charge, modern, breeze, by, book, pick-up service, shine, looking forward to-

Your Cool Stay in Jeju City Center!

Hello! Are you ready to discover a super fun place in Jeju City Center? Let's see what makes this place so awesome!

Our building is _____ and the room is a studio type, perfect for two people. It's a cool spot to stay right in the heart of Jeju City!

In your room, there's a big _____. Through this window, you can see Halla Mountain far away. Watching the sunset from here is really beautiful. It's like the sky is changing colors! The bedroom is small but has everything you need. There's a cozy bed where you can relax after a day of fun. Right next to it is a kitchen, where you can make snacks or small meals. And of course, there's a bathroom just for you.

If you want, we can make you a simple breakfast. Just let us know, and for a little extra _____, you'll start your day with something yummy.

Just a 5-minute walk away, there's a famous horse meat sushi restaurant. You should definitely try it!

We don't have a _____, but that's okay! There's a bus that comes straight from Jeju Airport to our place. Plus, a bus stop nearby takes you to Woljeongri Beach easily.

Please treat our home with care, just like your own. To keep the house comfortable for everyone, we can't allow pets.

Excited to _____ your adventure? Here's how:
- Email: jejucenterstay@cityadventures.com
- Call: +82 890 1234
- Instagram: @JejuCenterStay

We're _____ seeing you at our charming Jeju City Center place. It's going to be a great time!

Look at the picture. You are an owner of the place in Jeju. Now you are writing an Airbnb advertisement. The advertisement should include:

• title

• introduction

• details and features of the place

• house rules

• closing and contact information

• use *looking forward to* appropriately.

• use fronting sentence style appropriately.

GAPS

Genre		Audience	
Purpose		Style	

PREWRITING

DRAFT

FINAL DRAFT
61

CHECKLIST FOR REVISING AND EDITING
• Did I organize the text in an Airbnb advertisement style? _____ • Did I consider the direction of the gaze? _____ • Did I use fronting style sentences appropriately? _____ • Did I mention details and features of the place with adjectives to attract visitors? _____ • Did I use *looking forward to...*? _____ • Did I make a title keeping rules? _____ • Did I understand the procedures of pre-writing, drafting, revising, and editing? _____

Summative Assessment: Writing Portfolio Assignment (WPA)

INDEPENDENT WRITING	The purpose of this task is for you to practice advertisement writing.

You are an owner of the place in Jeju. Now you are writing an Airbnb advertisement. The advertisement should include:

• title

• introduction

• details and features of the place

• house rules

• closing and contact information

• use *looking forward to* appropriately.

• use fronting sentence style appropriately.

GAPS

Genre:		Audience:	
Purpose:		Style:	

PREWRITING

DRAFT

FINAL DRAFT

CHECKLIST FOR REVISING AND EDITING

• Did I organize the text in an Airbnb advertisement style? _____

• Did I consider the direction of the gaze? _____

• Did I use fronting style sentences appropriately? _____

• Did I mention details and features of the place with adjectives to attract visitors? _____

• Did I use *looking forward to...*? _____

• Did I make a title keeping rules? _____

• Did I understand the procedures of pre-writing, drafting, revising, and editing? _____

ADVERTISMENT RUBRIC FOR MODULE 7

BAND	GENRE FEATURES	COHERENCE AND COHESION	LEXICAL RESOURCE	GRAMMATICAL RANGE AND ACCURACY WITH ACTION + ING AND FRONTING SENTENCES	TASK ACHIEVEMENT
3	Correctly uses the typical structure of an Airbnb advertisement (e.g., introduction, description of the place, etc). Includes an appropriate title and details with adjectives to create vivid scenes.	The advertisement is well-organized, with clear connections between sentences, and uses the direction of the gaze and fronting style sentences.	Utilizes a simple range of vocabulary correctly and effectively, suitable for A1 level.	Uses basic grammatical structures, punctuation, *action + ing* as **adjectives, present participant** and **present continuous** and *looking forward to* accurately and effectively, with no or very few errors.	Fully completes the task by appropriately addressing all aspects of the advertisement writing prompt with simple yet accurate supporting ideas.
2	Partially includes advertisement genre features with adjectives, but some key elements may be missing or inadequately executed.	The advertisement is generally well-organized but may lack some coherence in sentence connections or the direction of the gaze and fronting style sentences.	Uses some suitable vocabulary but may lack variety or contain some words not used correctly.	Uses some punctuation, *action + ing* as **adjectives, present participant** and **present continuous,** and *looking forward to*, but may contain errors that sometimes obstruct understanding.	Partially completes the task by addressing some aspects of the prompt with a few relevant but simple supporting ideas; however, some aspects might be lacking.
1	Largely misses advertisement genre features, and includes inappropriate elements.	The advertisement is disorganized or lacks logical flow from one sentence to another.	Shows a lack of vocabulary variety or contains many words used incorrectly.	Lacks accuracy in the use of punctuation, *action + ing*, as **adjectives, present participant** and **present continuous,** and *looking forward to* making the instruction difficult to understand.	Largely fails to appropriately address the advertisement writing prompt or lacks the necessary supporting ideas.
0	The advertisement is not written				

Formative Evaluation: Teachers' diaries and records

Name of student (grade in school)		
Date	Diary	Record

Summative Evaluation: Student Survey Questionnaire

Rating scale questions		1 = "strongly disagree" 5 = "strongly agree"				
1	The goals of the course were clear and appropriate.	1	2	3	4	5
2	I was clearly stated my responsibilities and course requirements at the beginning.	1	2	3	4	5
3	The assessment used in the course was appropriate and fair.	1	2	3	4	5
4	The materials used in the course were appropriate and useful.	1	2	3	4	5
5	The texts and topics covered were interesting and relevant.	1	2	3	4	5
6	I was given clear instructions and explained things well.	1	2	3	4	5
7	I was given enough chances to write.	1	2	3	4	5
8	The lessons contained an appropriate variety of activities.	1	2	3	4	5
Open-ended questions						
9	What did you like most about the course?					
10	What did you like least about the course?					

Guided by Growth

This section provides a concise introduction to the key concepts and interrelations of TCL, genre writing, and process writing, which form the foundational methodology of this book. A thoughtful and thorough reading of this section is essential, as it will significantly benefit your understanding and participation in the class/

This document is a guide that provides a sample lesson plan to help teachers in their teaching process. Teachers don't have to follow it exactly, and it can be adjusted based on the teacher's experience and the needs of the students.

Using this guide could be very helpful for new teachers or those not very experienced with making lesson plans. It allows teachers to make their own lesson plans suitable for their students and their teaching situation.

This guide supports a detailed and effective way of planning lessons, making teachers more flexible and creative in their teaching strategies. This way, teaching becomes more focused on the students' needs, helping them learn in a way that's best for them.

Often, due to tight class schedules, instructors rush into lessons without clarifying the objectives. This lack of context is a key reason why students might not find the class engaging. By discussing questions and exchanging views with students, educators can leverage their existing knowledge and spark curiosity in the subject matter.

While many Korean English learners might not naturally choose to write diaries in English, I've included a diary module in this book for several reasons. Firstly, it's an excellent way to practice past tenses and improve coherence and cohesion. Many learners find it challenging to freely express their personal experiences and feelings in English, and the diary format can help break down these barriers. Plus, this module offers a chance to explore different ways of expressing time, rather than sticking to just one approach.

Learning keywords is a gradual process, not something that occurs instantly. A learner needs multiple exposures to a word to learn it effectively. The texts within a module generally reuse many of the words, facilitating this repetitive exposure. Additionally, there are more extensive learning resources available in the assignments towards the end of the book, which can be highly beneficial, so be sure to make good use of them. Most vocabulary learning focuses on linking words in Korean and English, but it's also crucial to remember the importance of learners consistently hearing the pronunciation and accent of essential words. Especially here, 'floor', 'ceiling', and 'modern' are words that are often mispronounced. In the case of 'floor', it is frequently pronounced as [flʊd]. For 'ceiling', due to unfamiliarity with the pronunciation rules of the vowels in 'c' and 'g', it is mostly pronounced as [ˈkiːlɪŋ]. Additionally, 'modern' is often pronounced as [ˈmɑːdən], which requires correction.

In this book, webtoons play a pivotal role in showcasing why this genre stands out uniquely. Instead of casually browsing through the webtoons, teachers should motivate learners by having them read in groups or participate in role-playing activities. Furthermore, guiding them through the webtoon dialogues will help them understand the essence of the genre and the book's overarching narrative

When learners are told to write according to the flow of their gaze, the majority suddenly become unaware of it because it has been too instinctive a focus for them. In this textbook, by guiding the flow of gaze with surrounding objects, learners should be made aware that this flow is not a rule to memorize but a natural progression. Such a living flow of gaze enhances the connectivity between sentences and has the effect of making the text form a picture in the reader's mind. Let's ensure that learners always keep the reader in mind when writing.

Let's ensure that learners familiarize themselves with each tip through practice exercises, thereby understanding the characteristics of the advertising genre. In particular, for tip 4, since learners find it more challenging to write details than expected, there is a need for teachers to guide them in using a variety of adjectives, adverbs, or their compounds.

Here, what we call "Common Sayings" are also widely recognized as "fixed expressions." Learning these as whole patterns, instead of dissecting their grammatical structures, can be more beneficial for learners. In the use of 'looking forward to', learners often make mistakes because they memorize it without distinguishing whether the 'to' is part of the infinitive or a preposition. In such cases, explaining that 'forward' carries the meaning of moving ahead, and thus the prepositional 'to' contributes a sense of direction towards something, can be very helpful to learners.

9 Verb+ing, like to-infinitive, has many meanings and uses. As explained in Volume 6, true learning occurs when students approach these not by studying grammatical terms but by understanding their use and meaning within sentences. Let's have learners themselves compare and analyze each sentence, discovering differences and determining which interpretation is more natural.

10 The fronting sentence structure might be very unfamiliar to Korean students. It is sometimes taught as an inverted form, but knowing the reason for its use is more important than such grammatical terminology. As explained in the text, it is simply to bring forward something important to emphasize it more. In my case, I teach the verb 'be' as an '='. Under the principle that 1+1=2 is the same as 2=1+1, I could see that students' understanding improved when explaining inversion in this manner.

[닫는 말]

Discover Writing Discover Korea 시리즈는 단순한 영어 학습서가 아닌, 한국 문화의 심장으로의 여행입니다. 이 시리즈 안에서 학습자들과 선생님들은 언어 학습과 문화적 몰입이 동시에 어우러진 독특한 경험을 할 수 있습니다. 일상 생활에서 먼 거리에 있던 그동안의 영어학습과 달리, 이 시리즈는 그 간극을 메워 교육적이면서도 공감 가능한 학습 경험을 제공합니다.

또한, 이 시리즈는 언어 학습에 새로운 시각을 제시합니다. 한국 문화, 관습 및 경험을 영어 교육에 엮음으로써 종합적인 접근 방식으로 언어를 습득할 기회를 제공합니다.

저는 여기에서 멈추지 않고 이 시리즈를 확장하고 한국 문화, 역사 및 현대 생활의 풍부함을 더 깊이 탐구하고 다른 장르로 확장할 계획이며 영어 쓰기교육을 넘어 읽기, 듣기 및 말하기를 포함한 종합적인 자료를 만들고 싶습니다.

흥미진진한 영어와 한국문화의 탐구 여정에 저와 함께 해보시면 어떨까요? 한 페이지 한 페이지마다 다양한 글의 장르와 한국을 탐험하면서 영어쓰기의 즐거움을 다시 발견해보세요. 독자가 되어 주심에 감사드리며, 앞으로의 만남을 기다리겠습니다.

2024 년 2 월 16 일

서은옥 드림

[Epilogue]

The **Discover Writing Discover Korea** series is not just a set of English textbooks; it's a journey into the heart of Korean culture. In these pages, you'll find a unique blend of language learning and cultural immersion. These books bridge the gap that feels distant from our daily lives, making the learning experience not only educational but also relatable.

It offers a fresh perspective on language learning. By weaving Korean culture, customs, and experiences into English education, it provides a holistic approach to language acquisition.

As for the future, my commitment is unwavering. I plan to expand this series, delving deeper into the richness of Korean culture, history, and modern life with other genres. I aim to create a comprehensive resource that not only enhances English writing skills but also reading listening and speaking, delving deeper into the richness of Korean culture, history, and modern life.

So, join me in this exciting journey of language and culture. Rediscover the joy of learning as you explore different genres and Korea, one page at a time. Thank you for your support, and I look forward to sharing more with you in the future.

Sincerely,

Eun-ok Seo

Discover Writing Discover Korea 7

발 행 | 2024년 8월 6일

저 자 | 서은옥

펴낸이 | 한건희

펴낸곳 | 주식회사 부크크

출판사등록 | 2014.07.15(제2014-16호)

주 소 | 서울특별시 금천구 가산디지털1로 119 SK트윈타워 A동 305호

전 화 | 1670-8316

이메일 | info@bookk.co.kr

ISBN | 979-11-410-9970-1

www.bookk.co.kr